Looking at Countries

CHINA

Jillian Powell

W
FRANKLIN WATTS
LONDON•SYDNEY

First published in 2006 by
Franklin Watts
338 Euston Road
London NW1 3BH

Franklin Watts Australia
Hachette Children's Books
Level 17/207 Kent Street
Sydney NSW 2000

ISBN-10: 0 7496 6481 9
ISBN-13: 978 0 7496 6481 7

Dewey classification: 915.1

Series editor: Sarah Peutrill
Art director: Jonathan Hair
Design: Rita Storey
Cover design: Peter Scoulding
Picture research: Diana Morris
Picture credits: Paul Barton/Corbis: 21. Claro Cortes
IV/Reuters/Corbis: 23. Bernd Ducke/Superbild/A1 Pix: 17, 26b.
Ric Ergenbright/Corbis: 15b. Haslin/Sygma/Corbis: 24. Jon
Hicks/Corbis: 11b, 18t, 20t. Earl & Nazima Kowall/Corbis: 12.
Bob Krist/Corbis: 9t. Photocuisine/Corbis: 20b. Carl & Ann
Purcell/Corbis: 15t. Keren Su/Corbis: 1, 7t. Keren Su/Lonely
Planet Images: 10. Superbild/A1 Pix: 6, 7b, 9b, 11t, 18b, 22, 25t,
26t. Superbild/Haga/A1 Pix: 13, 19, 25b. Superbild/Incolor/A1
Pix: front cover, 4, 8, 16, 27. Peter Turnley/Corbis: 14.

A CIP catalogue record for this book is available
from the British Library.

Printed in China

Contents

Where is China?

China is in eastern Asia. It is the fourth largest country in the world, after Canada, Russia and the United States of America.

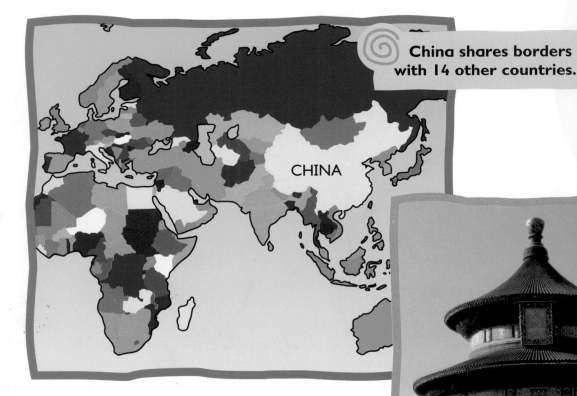

China shares borders with 14 other countries.

CHINA

The capital city, Beijing, is in north-eastern China. Beijing is one of the largest cities in China. Over 15 million people live there. The city is more than 3,000 years old. It has beautiful temples, palaces and parks alongside modern skyscraper buildings.

The Temple of Heaven in Beijing was built in 1420.

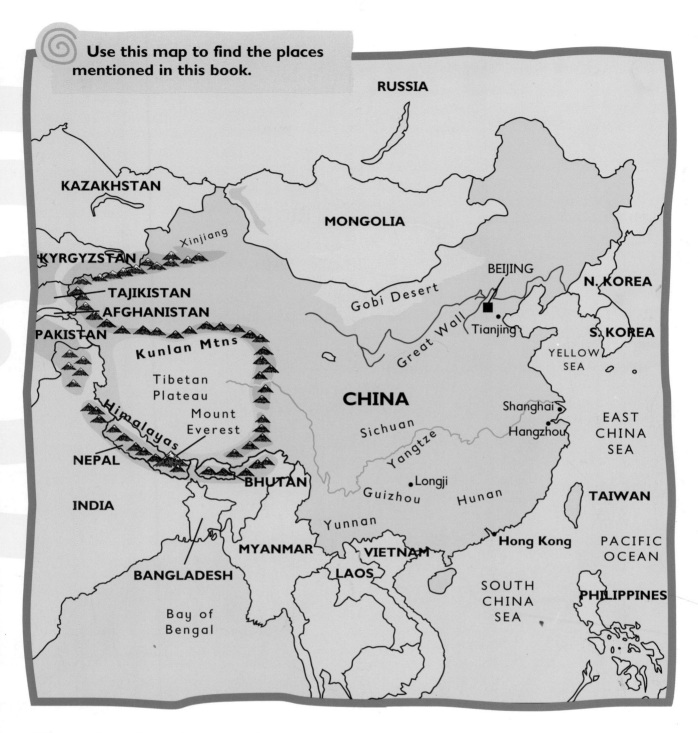

Use this map to find the places mentioned in this book.

RUSSIA

KAZAKHSTAN

MONGOLIA

Xinjiang

KYRGYZSTAN

TAJIKISTAN

AFGHANISTAN

PAKISTAN

Kunlan Mtns

Gobi Desert

BEIJING

N. KOREA

Great Wall

Tianjing

S. KOREA

YELLOW
SEA

Tibetan
Plateau

Mount
Everest

CHINA

Sichuan

Shanghai

Hangzhou

EAST
CHINA
SEA

Himalayas

NEPAL

BHUTAN

INDIA

Yangtze

Longji

Guizhou

Hunan

TAIWAN

Yunnan

MYANMAR

VIETNAM

Hong Kong

PACIFIC
OCEAN

BANGLADESH

LAOS

SOUTH
CHINA
SEA

PHILIPPINES

Bay of
Bengal

China has borders with countries including Russia, Mongolia and India. It has a coastline along the Pacific Ocean, the Yellow Sea, the East China Sea and the South China Sea.

Did you know?

The Chinese call their country *Zhongguo*, which means the Middle Kingdom.

The landscape

China has many different landscapes, including high snowy mountains, sandy deserts, rocky plains, sub-tropical forests and swamps.

The Great Wall of China stretches over 6,000 kilometres over mountains, deserts and river valleys. It was built to keep China's enemies out and took hundreds of years to finish.

The highest mountains are in the north and west. They enclose the Tibetan Plateau, a huge area of high land where little grows.

Did you know?

Mount Everest, which lies on the border of China and Nepal, is the world's highest mountain.

Less than one quarter of
China's land can be farmed.
Terraced fields are cut into
the hillsides for growing
crops including rice, tea and
vegetables. The most fertile
farmland is in central and
eastern China. Here there
are wide plains, and rivers
that bring water to the soil.

The Yangtze is the
longest river in China.

Weather and seasons

Much of China has a temperate climate, but there are big differences between the north and south.

In the north it is colder and drier. There is little rain and icy winds blow in from Siberia in winter. But in the Gobi Desert it can be very hot in summer (45°C) and bitterly cold in winter (-40°C).

Did you know?

Parts of northern China have snow for 150 days a year.

Camels are used to carry goods across the Gobi Desert.

People cool off in a fountain in Hong Kong in the south.

Most of the south has a tropical climate, with warm weather and plenty of rain all year round. But in the Himalayan mountain ranges of the south-west, the climate is sub-arctic. This means that the summers are short and the winters are long and cold.

In the summer monsoon season, between May and September, strong winds and heavy rains blow in from the Pacific Ocean. There can be typhoons on the south-east coast between July and September, causing damage and flooding.

A couple wearing the traditional folk dress of Tibet, where the climate is sub-arctic.

Chinese people

Over 1.3 billion people live in China. Most are Han Chinese, the people who have lived there for over 4,000 years. They speak Mandarin Chinese.

Did you know?

One in five people in the world are Chinese.

A crowd gathered for a festival in the Guizhou region.

There are also over 70 million people from other ethnic groups in China, including Mongolians, Tibetans, Zhuang, Jinuo and Miao. Each has their own language, culture, religion and traditional costume.

The Jinuo, from the mountains of Yunnan, are known for growing tea and weaving cloth.

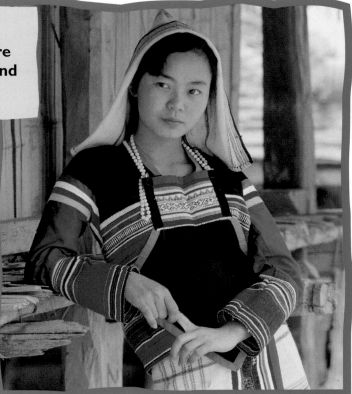

Traditions and ceremony are important in everyday life in China.

Some people practise folk religions. Others are Buddhists, Taoists, Muslims or Christians.

A group practise Tai Chi in a park in Shanghai. Taoists, and others, practise Tai Chi to keep their brain and body fit.

Family and school

Family is very important for most Chinese people. They have great respect for older people and for their ancestors. Grandparents often live with or near their families and help working parents by looking after the children.

At the festival of Ching Ming, families remember their ancestors and picnic by their graves.

These children are having a lesson at a primary school in Xinjiang in northern China.

Most children start school when they are six. Then they have nine years of education. The school day usually begins at 8 am and ends at 4 pm. Many schools have 10 minutes of physical exercise before classes, and children also enjoy games and sports after school.

Did you know?

Chinese children have their own festival called Children's Day on 1st June.

Country

More than two thirds of people in China live in villages and work in the countryside. Some people have small plots where they grow food for their families and a little to sell at market. They may keep a few animals such as a pig, and chickens or ducks for meat and eggs.

Did you know?

China grows more watermelons than any other country.

This couple, who live in the Sichuan region, are carrying pails of water for their crops.

These men are preparing flooded rice fields for sowing. They are using oxen, which are a kind of cattle.

Most farmers grow food for the Chinese state. They sow and harvest crops using hand tools and animals to help them. Some farms now have tractors for ploughing and taking food to market.

In the north, most farms grow crops such as wheat, millet or soya. South of the Yangtze River, where the climate is warmer and wetter, tea and rice are grown.

These women are harvesting tea in Hangzhou.

City

Just under a third of people in China live in cities. Many Chinese cities are very crowded, with several million people living there. The largest cities are the capital Beijing, Shanghai and Tianjing. They are busy, modern cities with lots of skyscraper buildings. These contain offices, homes, shops and restaurants.

This is a busy shopping street with skyscraper buildings in Shanghai.

Many people use bikes to get to work in Chinese cities.

Beijing, like all older cities in China, is built on a grid with streets running from east to west and north to south. It has long shopping streets, busy street markets, and old areas of narrow lanes called *hutongs*.

Did you know?

Tiananmen Square in Beijing is the largest public square in the world.

Chinese homes

In the crowded cities of China, most people live in small flats in skyscraper blocks. Some factories, companies and schools provide homes for their workers.

In old city centres, houses were traditionally built around courtyards leading off narrow lanes or *hutongs*. These can still be seen in Beijing.

Hong Kong workers live in these blocks of flats.

These traditional houses in Beijing are built around a courtyard with a small garden.

These old houses in the countryside in south China are built from the local stone.

In the country, most houses are single storey and are built from mud, clay bricks or stone. In places that often have floods, homes are built up on platforms to keep them dry.

Did you know?

Some people in China live in cave homes, others live on house-boats called *sampans*.

Food

Many kinds of fresh food are sold on markets like this one in Beijing.

Rice is a staple food in China, especially in the south. In the north, wheat is made into bread, noodles and dumplings called *jiaozi*.

Many regions have their own special dishes and styles of cooking. In Sichuan and Hunan, the food is hot and spicy. In the south, dishes include sweet and sour pork, and dim sum, which are dumplings made of flour and water that are steamed or fried.

Dim sum are often served in little baskets and eaten as snacks.

Chinese children learn how to use chopsticks from their parents and grandparents.

Steaming and stir-frying are popular methods of cooking in many parts of China. Meals are eaten with chopsticks and are often served in lots of small dishes. Sharing meals together is an important part of family life.

Did you know?

Chinese children eat noodles on their birthdays to bring them luck and a long life.

At work

About half the Chinese population work in farming. In the country, many people are poor as there is not enough work for everyone. Many younger people are moving to the cities to find jobs in factories or offices.

This woman is decorating a vase in a porcelain factory.

This factory makes plastics and chemicals.

Chinese factories make machinery, cars, aircraft, clothes, electronics, plastics and ceramics. There are large oil and gas factories and iron and steelworks.

There are also more and more jobs in cinemas, hotels, restaurants and shops in China's busy cities.

Did you know?

Chinese inventions include paper and fireworks.

Having fun

Chinese people like to keep fit. Badminton, volleyball, table tennis and kite flying are all popular sports in China. Most schools and factories have teams of players.

People also enjoy playing board and card games, such as Chinese chess and *mah-jong*.

Did you know?

Some Chinese kites are so large it takes several people to fly them.

Chinese people support their badminton team at the Olympic Games.

The Beijing Opera performs all over the world. Opera stars dress in colourful make-up and costumes.

Chinese opera, acrobats and circus performers are famous all round the world.

Festivals are celebrated with feasting, music, parades and fireworks. The most important festival is Chinese New Year, which is in January or February. Dancers dress as lions or dragons and parade through the streets.

Dragon dancers celebrate Chinese New Year.

China: the facts

• China is a Communist state, called the People's Republic of China. The President is head of the government and power is held by the leading members of the Communist Party.

The Chinese currency is the Yuan or the Renminbi – the people's currency.

The Chinese flag has yellow stars on a red background.

The Shanghai World Financial Centre is inside these tower buildings.

• China is divided into 23 provinces, 5 regions and 4 major cities. Each area has elected members of the National People's Congress, which is the Chinese Parliament.

• China is the fourth largest country in the world, and has the largest population, with over 1.3 billion people.

Did you know?

More people in the world speak Mandarin Chinese than any other language.

Glossary

Ancestors family members who lived long ago.

Ceramics objects made from fired clay or porcelain.

Chopsticks long sticks used for eating.

Communist a political party that is based on the idea that everything should belong to the state, rather than to each person.

Culture the ideas, beliefs and art of a people.

Electronics the industry that makes electrical goods.

Ethnic group people who share a common origin, culture or language.

Fertile rich and productive.

Hutongs narrow alleys.

Mah-jong a popular Chinese game played with sets of cards or tiles.

Monsoon seasonal winds carrying heavy rain.

Parliament a group of people who decide a country's laws.

Plateau an area of high, flat land.

Porcelain smooth, white pottery.

Staple food a basic food in the diet of a people.

Sub-arctic land found at the Arctic Circle or the type of climate which is like that found in the sub-arctic.

Sub-tropical land found close to the Tropics or the type of climate which is like that found in the Tropics.

Swamps flat, wet land that floods each year.

Taoist someone who follows the religion and beliefs of Taoism, based on the teachings of Lao-tze, who lived in the sixth century BCE.

Temperate never very hot or cold.

Terraced cut into raised flat banks.

Traditions ways and beliefs that have been passed down through generations.

Tropical belonging to the Tropics, part of the Earth near the Equator.

Typhoons violent tropical storms.

Find out more

www.gigglepotz.com/ china.htm
A children's site with lots of information, links and activities on China.

www.timeforkids.com/TFK/ hh/goplaces (click China)
A website with sections on sightseeing and a language section with some words to learn in Mandarin.

www.atozkidsstuff.com/ china.html
Lots of information on Chinese history and fun activities to do.

Note to parents and teachers: Every effort has been made by the Publishers to ensure that these websites are suitable for children, that they are of the highest educational value, and that they contain no inappropriate or offensive material. However, because of the nature of the Internet, it is impossible to guarantee that the contents of these sites will not be altered. We strongly advise that Internet access is supervised by a responsible adult.

Some Mandarin words

Mandarin Chinese is the main language of China. It is written with symbols called characters. Each one is a word or idea. There are about 50,000 characters to learn! There are three characters for the names of countries in the box below.

Speak some Mandarin:

English	Say ...
Excuse me	lao-jya
Hello	nee-hao
Goodbye	zai-jyen
No	boo-shir
Please	ching
Sorry	dway-boo-chee
Thank you	dor syair
Yes	shir
You're welcome	boo ker-chee

Some characters for countries:

中国	China
英国	Great Britain
美国	The USA

Some Mandarin words used in the English language:

Tea

Ketchup

Chopsticks

Silk

Japan

My map of China

Trace this map and use the map on page 5
to write the names of all the towns.

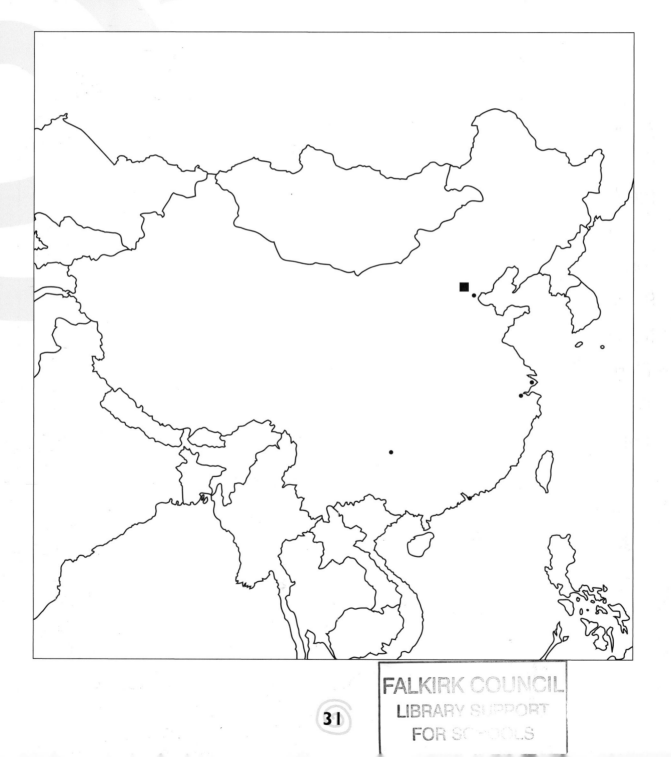

Index